E.P.L.

T1-BIR-621

Flemish Giant Rabbit

The World's Biggest Bunny

by Leon Gray

Consultant: Karen Sue Clouse
National Federation of Flemish Giant Rabbit Breeders

BEARPORT
PUBLISHING

New York, New York

Credits

Cover, © Lobke Peers/Shutterstock; TOC, © Eric Isselée/Shutterstock; 4–5, © Tammy Clark/www.countylinerabbitry.webs.com; 6, © Lucile Petit; 8, © Oregon Zoo/Michael Durham; 9, © Lynda Turcotte/www.serenovalleyrabbits.com and © s_oleg/Shutterstock; 10, © Lynda Turcotte/www.serenovalleyrabbits.com; 10, © Tammy Clark/www.countylinerabbitry.webs.com; 11, © karen claus/Shutterstock; 12, © Amandamhanna/Dreamstime.com; 13, © Lynda Turcotte/www.serenovalleyrabbits.com; 14–15, © Lewis Durham/Rex Features; 16, 17, 18, 19, © Lynda Turcotte/www.serenovalleyrabbits.com; 20, 21, © Tammy Clark/www.countylinerabbitry.webs.com; 22L, © ja/Wikipedia; 22C, © www.jennysrabbits.wordpress.com; 22R, © Oldhaus/Wikipedia; 23TL, © Tammy Clark/www.countylinerabbitry.webs.com; 23TR, 23BL, © Lynda Turcotte/www.serenovalleyrabbits.com; 22BR, © kotomiti/Shutterstock.

Publisher: Kenn Goin
Senior Editor: Joyce Tavolacci
Creative Director: Spencer Brinker
Photo Researcher: Calcium Creative
Produced for Bearport by Calcium Creative

Library of Congress Cataloging-in-Publication Data in process at time of publication (2013)
Library of Congress Control Number: 2012034285
ISBN-13: 978-1-61772-729-0 (library binding)

For more information, write to Bearport Publishing Company, Inc., 45 West 21st Street, Suite 3B, New York, New York 10010. Printed in the United States of America.

10 9 8 7 6 5 4 3 2 1

Contents

One Big Bunny

The Flemish giant rabbit is the biggest bunny in the world.

A Flemish giant rabbit can weigh as much as two large cats.

The Flemish giant rabbit can grow up to 2.6 feet (79 cm) long. That is about as long as a skateboard.

What's in a Name?

More than 150 years ago, people began raising Flemish giant rabbits.

The huge rabbits and their owners lived in Flanders, which is now part of Belgium.

The word *Flemish* means "from Flanders."

That is why these supersize bunnies are called Flemish giants.

In the past, Flemish giant rabbits were raised only for their fur and meat. Today, however, most owners keep them as pets.

Where Flemish Giant Rabbits Were First Raised

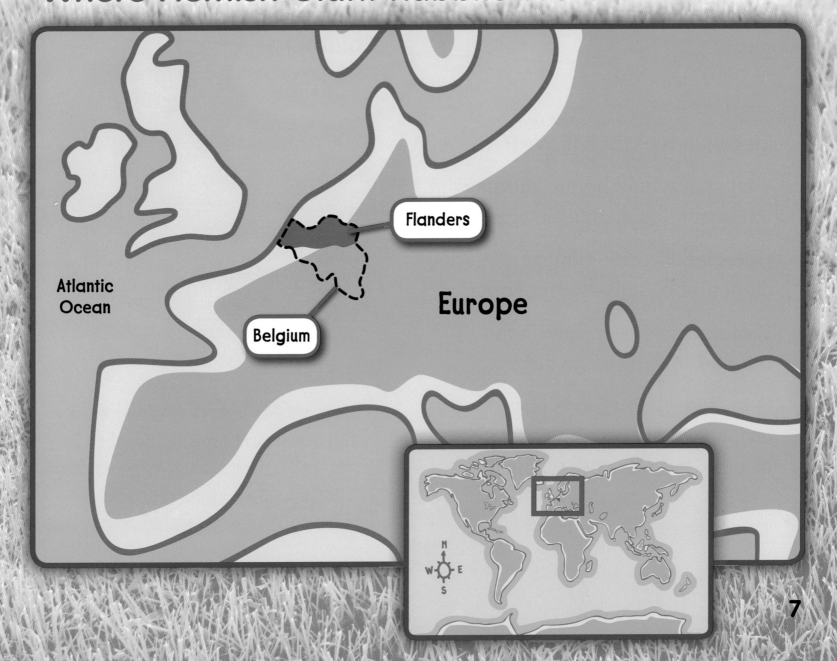

Flanders

Belgium

Atlantic Ocean

Europe

N
W E
S

Living with People

Many kinds of rabbits live in the wild.

They make their homes outdoors in tall grasses or in holes in the ground.

However, Flemish giant rabbits, like all pet rabbits, live with people.

Some owners keep their huge bunnies in extra-large cages.

Others let their rabbits hop around inside their homes or outside in fenced-in yards.

Columbia Basin pygmy rabbit

The Columbia Basin pygmy rabbit is the smallest wild rabbit in the world. It weighs about 1 pound (0.5 kg).

Large and Friendly

Although they are large, Flemish giant rabbits are usually gentle and friendly.

They like it when people pet their soft, fluffy **fur** and long ears.

As house pets, giant rabbits get along well with dogs and cats.

Some Flemish giant rabbits will even snuggle up with the family dog.

Flemish giant rabbits have short fur that can be gray, black, white, or light brown.

11

Handle with Care

Owners love to pick up and cuddle with their big bunnies.

However, they have to be careful.

If a rabbit does not like being held, it may nip or kick.

The best way to pick up a rabbit is to firmly hold its entire body and lift it.

That will help the rabbit feel safe and secure in a person's arms.

Flemish giant rabbits are most active early in the morning or at night. During the day, bunnies like to rest.

Feeding Time

Flemish giant rabbits have two big front teeth used for eating plants.

Bunnies like to eat dried grass called hay and leafy green **vegetables**, such as parsley or kale.

They love to munch on carrots, too.

Chewing crunchy foods keeps their teeth healthy and strong.

It is best for pet owners to put food for their Flemish giant rabbit in a heavy dish. That way their bunny cannot tip it over.

15

Squeaky Clean

Flemish giant rabbits spend a lot of time keeping themselves clean.

Like cats, they wash their fur with their tongues to get rid of dirt.

To clean their fuzzy ears, they pull them down across their face and lick them.

Owners can also help their bunnies look their best.

Once a week, they should brush their rabbits' fur to get rid of any old, loose hairs.

brushing

Flemish giant rabbits can easily be taught to go to the bathroom in a box, like a cat.

17

Rabbit Kits

A female Flemish giant rabbit has a **litter** of 5 to 12 **kits** at a time.

The babies are born with their eyes closed and little fur.

At first, the kits get all of their food by drinking milk from their mother's body.

After a few weeks, they open their eyes and start nibbling on food such as hay.

three-week-old kit

At birth, Flemish giant kits weigh 2.5 ounces (71 g), or about as much as a lemon. It can take up to one year for a baby to grow to its adult size.

Showing Off

Some owners enter their Flemish giant rabbits in shows.

To enter a show, each adult rabbit must be at least 13 pounds (6 kg).

The judge then looks at the animal's fur, ears, eyes, feet, and body shape.

The best-looking bunny is chosen as the winner!

Whether at home or in a show, Flemish giant rabbits are big and beautiful.

Some owners enter their rabbits in jumping races. The rabbit that jumps over several fences fastest wins.

More Big Rabbits

Flemish giant rabbits are part of a large group of animals called mammals. Almost all mammals give birth to live young instead of laying eggs. The babies drink milk from their mothers. Mammals are also warm-blooded and most have hair or fur on their skin.

Here are three more big rabbits that people keep as pets.

Checkered Giant Rabbit

The checkered giant rabbit can weigh up to 16 pounds (7.3 kg).

Continental Giant Rabbit

The continental giant rabbit also weighs up to 16 pounds (7.3 kg).

Giant Angora Rabbit

The giant angora rabbit can weigh more than 10 pounds (4.5 kg).

Flemish Giant Rabbit
20 pounds/9 kg

Checkered Giant Rabbit
16 pounds/7.3 kg

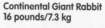

Continental Giant Rabbit
16 pounds/7.3 kg

Giant Angora Rabbit
10 pounds/4.5 kg

Glossary

fur (FUR) the soft, thick hair of certain animals

litter (LIT-ur) a group of baby animals that are born to the same mother at the same time

kits (KITS) baby rabbits

vegetables (VEJ-tuh-buhlz) parts of a plant that animals or people can eat

23

Index

Read More

Royston, Angela. *Rabbit (Baby Animals)*. North Mankato, MN: Chrysalis Education (2005).

Walker, Kathryn. *See How Rabbits Grow*. New York: PowerKids Press (2009).

Zobel, Derek. *Rabbits (Blastoff! Readers: Backyard Wildlife)*. Minneapolis, MN: Bellwether Media (2011).

Learn More Online

To learn more about Flemish giant rabbits, visit
www.bearportpublishing.com/EvenMoreSuperSized